CHURCH MUSIC SOCIETY PUBLICATION: 023A
Hon. General Editor: Richard Lyne

CONC

T0033735

for the Choir and Congregation of St. Mary's Church, North Leigh, Oxon...

Saint Mary's Mass

Music by ANTHONY CÆSAR

Kyrie

Alternative version of Kyrie

Gloria

For you — a-lone are the Ho - ly One, you a-lone are the Lord,—

you a-lone are the Most High, Je - sus Christ, with the Ho - ly Spi - rit,

in the glo - ry of God— the Fa - ther. A - men. A - men.

Gospel Responses

Glo - ry to Christ— our Sa - viour.

Praise — to Christ — our Lord. —

Sanctus – Benedictus

Ho - ly, Ho - ly, Ho - ly Lord, God — of pow'r and

might, heav'n — and earth are full— of your glo - ry. Ho-san-na in the

high - est. Bless - ed is he who comes — in the name — of the

Lord. Ho-san - na in the high - est, Ho - san - na in the high - est.

Acclamations

Agnus Dei

Acknowledgment

The *Gloria*, the *Sanctus*, the *Benedictus* and the *Agnus Dei* from *The Order for Holy Communion Rite A* from the Alternative Service Book 1980 are © International Consultation on English Texts and are reproduced with permission of the Central Board of Finance of the Church of England.

Origination by Jeanne Fisher, Ludlow, Shropshire
Printed by Halstan & Co. Ltd., Amersham, Bucks

Pack of 10 copies
Not available separately

ISBN 0-19-395363-3

9 780193 953635